erka...

ADA Programming Success In A Day
By Sam Key

Beginner's guide to fast, easy and efficient learning of ADA programming

2nd Edition

Table of Contents

Introduction

I want to thank you and congratulate you for purchasing the book, *"ADA Programming Success in a day: Beginner's guide to fast, easy and efficient learning of ADA programming"*.

This book contains proven steps and strategies on how to use ADA. This beginner's guide will teach you the following:

- History of ADA
- ADA Basic language
- Ada Packages
- And so much more

After this book, you will get to understand one of the seemingly complex but incredibly easy to use programming languages.

.

Thanks again for purchasing this book, I hope you enjoy it!

Chapter 1 Ada History

Ada is a programming language created to handle large and long-lived applications, specifically embedded systems. This modern programming platform provides the efficiency and reliability that these applications require.

The programming language was first developed in the early years of the 1980s, a version called Ada 83. The language was developed by a team in France, at the CII-Honeywell-Bull and headed by Dr. Jean Ichbiah. The programming language was later revised in the 1990s, by a team led by Tucker Taft of Intermetrics (US). This revised version is called Ada 95, which became the first object-oriented language to receive an ISO, which meant it was internationally standardized. Ada 95 underwent a minor revision under the mandates of the ISO, and the latest version was named Ada 2005. Currently, Ada is undergoing some revisions to include support for annotations to the program and some additional features.

"Ada" is not actually an acronym. It is a real name of a real person. The name was in honor of a lady mathematician, Augusta Ada Lovelace. She was widely considered as the first programmer in the world, largely because of her work with the equally renowned Charles Babbage. Ada Lovelace was also Lord Byron's daughter.

How Ada Started

The Ada computer programming language was developed through the most expensive and extensive effort ever made in the history of computer programming.

It all started with the US Department of Defense. The DoD was using embedded systems for most of its applications. There were more than 450 different programming languages for the numerous applications of the DoD. None of these were standardized. That meant high inefficiency and unreliability. The DoD rarely reused software because of this. Hence, there was constant need for newer software and upgrades. The Air Force, Navy, and Army proposed to have a high-level programming language developed specifically for embedded systems.

In 1977, the specifications for Ada's language design were completed. There were 4 contractors who submitted their proposals chosen for Phase I of the programming language design. A 2-month evaluation followed, which trimmed down the proposals into the 2 best language designs. The decision was a result of an evaluation made by 400 volunteers, which were divided into 80 teams. In the phase, Phase II, another evaluation was made. After 2 grueling years, in May 1979, the chosen language design was the one made by CII Honeywell/Bull, which, incidentally, was the only foreign contractor for the entire project. This goes to show how rigorous the process was until the final Ada language design was approved. CII Honeywell/Bull was given the permission to continue on to Phase III. The language design was published by ACM, and in a few months, more than 500 reports from 15 countries were received. These were evaluations and recommendations about the new programming language. The collected reports gave a few minor changes but none were real drastic. These suggestions were all taken into consideration to create the final and official version of Ada, more commonly referred to as Ada 83. This programming language was frozen in the succeeding 5 years.

Important Language Features

The most notable features of Ada program are the following:

Packages

Packages are encapsulated data objects, procedure specifications and data types. These support the data abstraction program design.

Exception handling

This program language is excellent capabilities for exception handling. This allows Ada to run and handle run-time errors on its own.

Generic Program Units

Procedures can be written without having to define data types. This is because Ada offers generic units that can be used for creating any program.

Concurrent/Parallel Processing

Tasks in Ada programming language can be executed as concurrent or parallel.

Areas for Ada Application

Ada has numerous applications beyond the originally intended tasks for the different needs of the US Department of Defense. Over the years, more and more applications and advantages of using Ada are being discovered. Worldwide, this programming language is known for its excellent reliability and efficiency when it comes to domains that require high security. Domains that are highly sensitive, which are critical when it comes to safety and require high integrity also turn to Ada for all these requirements. This includes:

- Medical devices

- Air traffic control

- Commercial aircraft avionics

- Military avionics

- Railroad systems

- Banking systems

- Manufacturing industry

- Communication systems

- Commercial aviation

- Computer-aided design

Chapter 2 ADA Language and Uses

Ada programming embodies modern principles in software engineering. It proves to be an excellent programming language when teaching and learning introductory as well as advanced courses in computer science. In the field of real-time technologies, Ada plays a central role.

Overview of Ada Language

This programming language is multi-faceted. It is a versatile, with a stack-based, classical, general purpose language. It is not limited to any particular development methodology. The syntax is simple and the controlled statements are structured. Facilities for data composition are flexible. Type checking is strong and efficient, incorporating the conventional code modularization features or subprograms. It also has exception handling, which is a system that detects and appropriately responds to exceptional run-time conditions.

These basic features come with much more functions:

Scalar ranges

Programmers that use Ada find it easy and simple to clearly specify the range of values allowed for scalar types of values such as enumeration, fixed-type, floating point or integer types. When a program is run with a value that is out of range for that type, it will produce a run-time error. With Ada, specifying the constraints on value range makes the programmer intent more specific. This way, it is easier to detect any major source of user input or coding errors.

Programming at large

Ada 83, the original programming language design, pioneered package construct. This feature allows data encapsulation or information hiding. It also supported modularization. These provided developers control over the namespace accessible within any of the given compilation units. The succeeding version,

Ada 95, introduced "child units", which considerably added flexibility. This feature also eased very large system designs.

Ada 2005 extended its modularization facilities, through mutual references allowed between different package specifications. This made it much easier to interface with other programming languages such as Java.

Generic Templates

Ada is able to meet the requirements for reusable components through its unique generics facility. Modules are parameterized in relation to the type of data and other entities of a particular program, like stack packages for a type of arbitrary element. With Ada's generics, parameterization happens at compile time, which does not penalize run-time performance.

OOP (Object-Oriented Programming)

Ada 83 was originally object-based. It allowed partitioning systems into modules to correspond to abstract types of data or objects. Since the original language, full OOP was not provided because there seemed no real importance for it in the real-time domain, which was Ada's main intent. Another reason for the absence of full OOP support is the issue of automatic garbage collection. OOP languages require an automatic garbage collection and this would majorly interfere with the desired efficiency and predictability of the Ada language.

But, GUIs and other components are fairly common in large real-time systems. These components do not have any real-time constraints and would function at optimum efficiency with OOP features. For this, Ada 95 came with a comprehensive OOP support via the "tagged Type" feature. This includes polymorphism, dynamic bonding, inheritance and classes. This still does not require automatic garbage collection. Rather, Ada 95 provides definitional features that allow supplying of "finalizations" or type-specific storage reclamation operations. Ada 2005 provides additional features for its OOP, such as interfaces that resemble the one in Java and a few traditional operations on invocation notation.

Ada is basically neutral methodology. It does not impose any distributed overhead for its OOP. This feature only comes into play is an application requires it. If it does not, then the features for OOP need not have to be used, without any penalty for run-times.

Concurrent programming

Concurrency is supplied with high-level, structured facility. The concurrency unit for Ada is called a "task", which in itself is a program entity. Tasks implicitly communicate through shared data. These can also communicate explicitly through synchronous control mechanism called a rendezvous. Shared data items are abstractly defined as "protected objects". This feature was made available by Ada 95. These have operations that can be called upon from multiple tasks via execution under mutual exclusion.

Ada also supports asynchronous task interactions, particularly on task termination and timeouts. During certain operations, asynchronous behavior is deferred in order to avoid having to leave shared data under inconsistent states. In Ada 2012 (latest version), several mechanisms were designed and put in place to aid in getting better use of multi-core architectures.

Systems Programming

All the necessary features that allows programmer to be closer to the hardware are supplied in Ada, whether in the Systems Programming Annex or in the core language. For instance, programmers can specify bit layouts for a field contained in a record, or place any data in specified machine addresses. Ada also allows for expressing either time-critical or specialized code sequences in the assembly language or specifying bit layouts for fields contained in a record. Interrupt handlers can also be written in Ada by using protected facility type.

Real Time Programming

Tasking features in Ada allows for the expression of the commonly used real-time idioms such as event-driven tasks or periodic tasks. Ada also has a Real-Time Annex that provides numerous facilities allowing programmers to prevent any unbounded priority inversions. Protected objects have locking policies defined with priority ceilings. Ada supports this ad allows for exceptionally efficient implementation. Mutexes are not even required. Ada does not allow protected operations to block. In Ada 95, task dispatching policy is defined. This requires tasks to continually run until it is either preempted or blocked. In Ada 2005, there is more of this kind, such as Earliest Deadline First.

High Integrity Systems

Ada places a huge emphasis on the principles of sound software engineering principles. This allows Ada to be able to support high-integrity application development, such as those requiring certification for safety standards (e.g., DO-178B) and security standards (e.g. Common Criteria). Strong typing inputs data that is intended for a single purpose will be inaccessible if the operations called forth is inappropriate. This prevents errors from occurring, such as when pointers are treated as integers. Ada has an array bounds checking that prevents vulnerabilities from buffer overrun. This is a very common occurrence in C and C++ programming languages.

There are instances when the full language becomes inappropriate in applications that are safety-critical. The flexibility and generality of this kind of application can interfere with traceability and certification requirements. Ada language addresses this concern with a compiler directive. This is called the pragma Restrictions. It allows programmers to constrain the features of the programming language to clearly defined subset. For instance, programmers that create constraints that exclude dynamic facilities of the OOP.

Ada's evolution is an unrelenting pursuit in increasing the language support capabilities for high-security and safety-critical applications. A few highlights of this include:

- Ada 2005: standardization of Ravenscar Profile, which is a compilation of concurrency features that are powerful and adequate to use for real-time programming but remain simple enough for practical certification.

- Ada 2012: introduced annotation facilities that can be used to add pre-conditions and post conditions, as well as invariants to various programs. These are useful as input for tools in static analysis and for checking run-times.

Benefits of Ada Programming Language

Numerous advantages are experienced with the use of Ada programming language:

- Helps in designing reliable and safe codes

- Reduces the cost of development

- Supports changes and advancements in technology

- Assists in complex program development

- Enables codes to be portable and readable

- Lowers the certification cost for software that are safety-critical

Summary of Features

- Object-oriented

- Strong typing

- Supports abstractions to fit the program domain

- Contains generic programming templates

- Exception handling

- Supports facilities required for code modular organization

- Contains standard libraries for string handling, containers, numeric computing and I/O

- Real-time programming

- Concurrent programming

- Numeric processing

- Distributed systems programming

- Supports interface with other programming languages such as C, Fortran and COBOL

The best thing about the Ada programming language is that it has proven to be a very powerful tool for addressing the various and actual issues that software developers face. It is now widely used among several major industries that design specific software for protecting business and lives.

Chapter 3 ADA Language Definitions

There are many terms use in Ada programming language. It helps to be familiar with these before making any programs.

Identifier

An identifier refers to objects used in Ada. Forming identifiers follow a few rigid rules to make sure that objects are well defined and to minimize errors. The most important guidelines include:

- Identifiers must always start with any of the letters of the English alphabet.

- After the starting letter, identifiers can contain as much numbers, underlines and letters. Just make sure that underlines only occur once in the identifier. Also, underlines must ever be the last character in the identifier.

- Letter cases are not very important.

- There are no limits to how long an identifier is. However, it is imperative for an identifier to fill one text line. The compiler writer may also impose limit on line length. Minimum length must be 200 characters or more.

- Special characters or blanks cannot be included in any identifier.

Some examples of identifiers include:

Ada	Valid identifier
ADA	valid; same as above because the case of the characters does not matter
Ada_Compiler	descriptive identifier
The_Year1998	descriptive identifier
a6b5c4d3e2f1	nondescript but still valid
10_days	invalid; identifiers must always start with a letter

13

```
Hello_guys_10
```
illegal; contains multiple underlines

```
Hello guys 10
```
illegal; contains blank spaces

```
"Theme"_88
```
illegal; contains special characters ("")

Selecting Identifiers

Identifiers need to be written correctly and should be meaningful and usable. The original design of the Ada program is "written once, read several times". Hence, the program requires easy-to-understand identifiers that instantly give the programmer or reader information. For example,

```
Test_results
    Basic_salary
    Participants_list
```

These examples have instant meanings, which are easier to work with, than identifiers that give no clue to what they are about at all. Consider these examples:

```
Vysn177863
    Syn12hj9
```

There are a few programmers that choose to use coded identifiers. However, this method will require a code reference, which can make it a little inconvenient on several points. This can really become a concern if a non-trivial program is being developed by a team. This might something of a personal choice if a program is meant not be shared or to make it difficult for unauthorized people to study the program.

Long identifiers, at first, will seem quite tedious and unappealing. This can be an issue when writing a program is under time-constraint. But such tedious task proves to be advantageous later on.

Long identifiers are easier to read the logic of the program is easy to understand.

Reserved Words

Reserved words are identifiers that Ada has already declared for specific purposes. These words cannot be used for purposes other than what Ada has intended them to be. There are 69 reserved words in Ada 95, 63 for Ada 83.

Reserved words help to simplify the task of writing Ada compilers. Writing compilers tend to be an enormous task because Ada is a large programming language and contains numerous cross checks and options. These reserved words can also help in making the final program easier to read and to understand.

Case Conventions

In Ada, programmers have the freedom to use any case for the alphabetic characters used when creating identifiers. There is practically numerous means of mixing the characters up. However, good programmers follow a few conventions, which help make the program easily read and understood. A well-balanced and intelligible use of cases would be more effective in conveying what the identifier is all about.

Reserved words: All of Ada's reserved words are written in the lower case.

Variables: All the variables should be written in lower case, but each word must always start with a capital letter.

Types: All the types in Ada program must have all its characters written in uppercase

Constraints: All the characters of all constants must be written in uppercase.

Enum Values: All the characters of enumerated values must be written in the uppercase (capital letters).

Attributes: All of the characters used in all attributes within the Ada program language must all be in capital letters.

Procedure names: All of the names of the different procedures must always start with a letter written in the uppercase (capital letter). All the succeeding characters are written in lower case.

This guideline applies when writing Function names, Package names and Library names.

Basic Definitions

There are lots of terms that will be in use as one progresses with the Ada programming language. Here are some of the basic ones that are critical to understand.

Exceptions

In other programming language, if a fatal run-time error occurs, the reaction is to abort the program. In real-time language, this is something very unacceptable. The program must continue to run, and, if possible, correct the error while the program is still running. An exception in Ada is any error or exceptional condition arising during program execution. Properly written Ada programs have the capability for defining what to do whenever error or exceptional conditions occur and still continue its operation.

Renaming

Programmers are allowed to assign new names to several program entities for convenience. The Ada language allows renaming task entries, exceptions, subprograms and objects. The new given name is, however, simply an alias, which provides a more meaningful label or name to the entity.

Overloading

Programmers using Ada are allowed to use a single name over and over for a number of varying items. Ada is smart enough to identify the difference. For example, "She used a block to block the door". The word "block" is used twice, but with different meanings. Each meaning depends on how the word was used. In this case, the 1st "block" meant something solid and the 2nd "block" meant to bar or obstruct the door. Ada uses this same method to differentiate the entity required, even if the same name is used for different entities. It has the smartness that can be relied on for this matter.

From these basic information, one can now see that Ada programming language may seem too complicated, tedious and overwhelming to study. But, there are also features that allow programmers to use the language in a much more convenient way.

Chapter 4 Elements of the Ada Programming Language

The Ada program also uses the same elements as other similar languages. There are variables, integers, strings and so on.

VARIABLES

Before any variable can be used anywhere in the program, it must be declared first. To do this:

```
VariableName : DataType;
```

Declaring starts by giving the variable a name. The name should consist of one word. If the desired name is more than just a word, write it without any spaces in between. For example, the desired variable name is "Quality Support Team". When declaring, write this variable name as "QualitySupportTeam".

Also, when giving names to variables, the first character must be a letter. The name can be a combination of different characters, such as letters, underscores and numbers, but always start with a letter. But, never use any special characters such as asterisk (*) or parenthesis. For example, variable names may be:

```
AnnaGradesQ1

SalaryQ1Q2

TaxExemptionFormula

Projected_Trajectory1
```

To declare more than 1 variable with each variable in its own line, this formula is used:

```
VariableName1 : DataType1;

VariableName2 : DataType1;
```

To declare more than 1 variable of the same data type, use this formula:

```
VariableName1, VariableName2 : DataType1;
```

The variables are declared within the same line. The variable names are separated by commas.

While any name and any combination of letters, underscores and numbers are allowed, there are some words that should not be used as variable names. Ada has "reserved words", which have already been predefined. These reserved words are:

abort	delay	in	pragma	synchronize
abs	delta	interface	private	tagged
abstract	digits	is	procedure	task
accept	do	limited	protected	terminate
access	else	loop	raise	then
aliased	elsif	mod	range	type
all	end	new	record	until
and	entry	null	rem	use
array	exception	not	renames	when
at	exit	of	requeue	while
begin	for	or	return	with
body	function	others	reverse	xor
case	generic	out	select	
constant	goto	overriding	separate	
declare	if	package	subtype	

After declaring, variables should be initialized. This step assigns values to the declared variables. This is necessary before the variable can be used. There are 2 options in initializing variables:

```
VariableName : DataType := Value;
```

This formula is used when declaring and initializing at the same time.

```
VariableName : DataType

begin

    VariableName:= Value;

end
```

This formula is used when the variable has already been declared and initializing is done afterwards.

The Keyword "declare"

The keyword "begin" is used in simultaneously declaring a variable within the body of a procedure. Before a variable is used, use the keyword to start the section where the variable is to be used. Then, incorporate the necessary code and finish the section with the keyword "end".

Take a look at this example:

```
with Ada.Text_IO;
use Ada.Text_IO;

procedure Practice is

begin
    declare
        -- Declarations
    begin
        -- Initializations
    end;
end Practice;
```

DATA TYPES

Like in every other programming language, Ada also incorporates several types of data in its programs.

Characters

Digits, letters and symbols are considered characters in the Ada language. The "character" keyword is used when declaring a variable designed to hold a variable. To initialize this data type, the value is written within single quotes ('...').

Consider this example:

```
with Ada.Text_IO;
use Ada.Text_IO;

procedure Introduction is
    status : character := 'S';
begin
    Put_Line("Status = " & character'image(status));
end Introduction;
```

The result will be printed as:

```
Status = 'S'
```

The "Put_Line" portion of the program is needed in order to display the value of the variable.

Strings

Strings refer to combination of characters. That is, any group of letters, digits and symbols written together in a single line- much like a phrase or a sentence. In Ada language, **String** data types represent these strings. Declare the variable first. Then, to initialize it, write the value it within double-quotes ("...").

```
with Ada.Text_IO;
use Ada.Text_IO;

procedure Introduction is
    sentence : String := "Experience amazing things
with Ada programming!";

begin

end Introduction;
```

21

To declare and display the value of this string variable, place the value and the variable name within the parenthesis of the "Put_Line" section.

```
with Ada.Text_IO;
use Ada.Text_IO;

procedure Practice is
      sentence : String := "Experience amazing things
with Ada programming!";

begin
      Put_Line(sentence);
end Practice;
```

The printed result will be:

```
Experience amazing things with Ada programming!
```

Concatenating Strings

In Ada programming, performing programs will often involve using strings that are added to each other. This step is called concatenating. To perform this type of operation, use the operator "**&**".

```
with Ada.Text_IO;
```

```
use Ada.Text_IO;

procedure Practice is
begin
     Put_Line("Raspberry" & "Cake");
end Practice;
```

The printed result is

```
RaspberryCake
```

Ada allows concatenating as many strings as possible.

```
with Ada.Text_IO;
use Ada.Text_IO;

procedure Practice is
begin
     Put_Line("Dessert Name: " & " Raspberry" & " " &
"Cake");
end Practice;
```

String variables can also be concatenated.

```
with Ada.Text_IO;
use Ada.Text_IO;

procedure Practice is
     DessertName1 : String := "Raspberry ";
     DessertNAme2 : String := "Cake ";

begin
     Put_Line(DessertName1 & DessertName2);
end Practice;
```

String variables and constant strings can be concatenated as well.

```
with Ada.Text_IO;
use Ada.Text_IO;

procedure Practice is
     DessertName1 : String := "Raspberry";
     DessertName2 : String := "Cake";

begin
     Put_Line("DessertEntree: " & DessertName1 & " : &
DessertName2);
end Practice;
```

Integers

Integers are numeric values for natural numbers. The integral value is represented in Ada programming using an **integer** data type.

```
with Ada.Text_IO;
use Ada.Text_IO;

procedure Practice is
     number : integer;

begin

end Practice;
```

To initialize the integer variable and assign it a numeric value that has no special characters:

```
with Ada.Text_IO;
use Ada.Text_IO;

procedure Practice;
     number : integer := 3141678

begin

end Practice;
```

In order to print or display the numerical value of an integer variable, place the desired result within the parentheses of the section **Put_Line()**. For this, enter **natural'image()** and then the variable name inside the parenthesis.

```
with Ada.Text_IO;
use Ada.Text_IO;

procedure Practice is
    number : integer := 3141678

begin
    Put_Line("Number: " & natural'image(number));
end Practice;
```

The printed result will be:

```
Number : 3141678
```

Natural numbers may also include underscores. However, the final and printed value will be as if the underscore was not there at all.

```
with Ada.Text_IO;
use Ada.Text_IO;

procedure Practice is
    number : Integer := 31416_78;

begin
    Put_Line("Number: " & natural'image(number));
end Practice;
```

Natural numbers written in the scientific format is also supported in the Ada program. For this, use the characters E or e to designate the scientific format of the natural number.

```
with Ada.Text_IO;
use Ada.Text_IO;

procedure Introduction is
     value1 : integer := 3970;
     value2 : integer := 563_290;
     value3 : integer := 439E4;
begin
     Put_Line("Value 1 = " & integer'image(value1));
     Put_Line("Value 2 = " & integer'image(value2));
     Put_Line("Value 3 = " & integer'image(value3));
end Introduction;
```

The displayed results will be

```
Value 1 = 3970
Value 2 = 563290
Value 3 = 4390000
```

Floating Point Numbers

Floating point numbers are numerical values that have decimals to separate some of the number components. When using the US English system, the period is used to separate the decimal values from the whole numbers. For example, 57.02 and 3.1416.

The keyword **float** is used when declaring decimal numbers. To initialize these values, include 1 decimal separator when assigning the number.

```
with Ada.Text_IO;
use Ada.Text_IO;

procedure Introduction is
    value : float := 56.25;
begin
    Put_Line ("Value = " & float'image(value));
end Introduction;
```

Like in natural numbers, floating numbers can also be declared with underscores.

```
with Ada.Text_IO;
use Ada.Text_IO;

procedure Introduction is
    value1 : float := 56.25_79;
    value2 : float := 34.55;
begin
    Put_Line ("Value 1 = " & float'image(value1));
    Put_Line ("Value 2 = " & float'image(value2));
end Introduction;
```

Scientific formats for floating point numbers are also supported. The letters e or E represents the scientific notation.

```
with Ada.Text_IO;
use Ada.Text_IO;

procedure Introduction is
    value1 : float := 56.25_79;
    value2 : float := 34.55;
    value3 : float := 64.3E7;
begin
    Put_Line ("Value 1 = " & float'image(value1));
    Put_Line ("Value 2 = " & float'image(value2));
    Put_Line ("Value 3 = " & float'image(value3));
end Introduction;
```

The printed display will be:

```
Value 1 = 5.625790E+01
Value 2 = 3.455000E+01
Value 3 = 6.470000E+07
```

27

Declaring sections with float point numbers follows this sample procedure:

```ada
with Ada.Text_IO;
use Ada.Text_IO;

procedure Practice is

begin
    declare
        number : Float;
    begin
        number := 503.15;

        put_line("Number = " & Float'Image(number));
    end;
end Practice;
```

For specifying precision:

```ada
with Ada.Text_IO, Ada.Float_Text_IO;
use Ada.Text_IO, Ada.Float_Text_IO; --, Example;

procedure Practice is
    type Natural_Number is Range 1 .. 100;
    number : Natural_Number;

    type Decimal_Number is digits 2;
    Single : Decimal_Number;

    DecNbr : Float;

begin
    number := 85;
    Single := 8.5;
    DecNbr := 45.5213;

    Put("Number = ");
    Put(Natural_Number'Image(number)); New_Line;
    Put("Decimal = ");
    Put(Decimal_Number'Image(Single)); New_Line;
    Put("Decimal = ");
    Put(DecNbr, Fore => 4, Aft => 2, Exp => 0);
New_Line;
    Put("Decimal = ");
    Put(DecNbr, Fore => 4, Aft => 2, Exp => 3);
New_Line;
    end Practice;
```

The displayed values will be:

```
Number = 85
Decimal = 8.5E+00
Decimal = 45.52
Decimal = 4.55E+01
```

CONSTANTS

Values that do not change are called constants. This is created using the keyword **constant**.

```
VariableName : constant DataType := Value;
```

To use this in a procedure, look at this programming exercise:

```
with Ada.Text_IO;
use Ada.Text_IO;

procedure Introduction is
     value1, value2 : integer;
     value3 : constant integer := 732;
begin
     value1 := 43867;
     value2 := 4228;

     Put_Line("Value 1 = " & integer'image(value1));
     Put_Line("Value 2 = " & integer'image(value2));
     Put_Line("Value 3 = " & integer'image(value3));
end Introduction;
```

Any variable can be turned into a constant. Just remember to assign values to the variables during its declaration in order to turn it into a constant.

```
with Ada.Text_IO;
use Ada.Text_IO;

procedure Introduction is
      InvoiceNumber : constant integer := 688534;
      InvoiceName   :  constant  String  :=  "Q1  Repair
Expenses";

      begin
      Put_Line("Invoice           #:            "            &
integer'image(InvoiceNumber));
           Put_Line("Full Name: " & InvoiceName);
      end Introduction;
```

After the constant is created, new values cannot be assigned to it anymore. Attempting to do o will result in an error message, just like in this example:

```
with Ada.Text_IO;
use Ada.Text_IO;

procedure Introduction is
      value1, value2 : integer;
      value3 : constant integer := 732;
begin
      value1 := 43867;
      value2 := 4228;
      value3 :=63553;

      Put_Line("Value 1 = " & integer'image(value1));
      Put_Line("Value 2 = " & integer'image(value2));
      Put_Line("Value 3 = " & integer'image(value3));
      end Introduction;
```

Notice that the line `value3 :=63553;` was added when it shouldn't because value3 was already declared previously as a constant (`value3 : constant integer := 732;`). The displayed result will be an error.

Also, when creating constants, the data type does not have to be specified if the constant's value is already a number.

```ada
with Ada.Text_IO;
use Ada.Text_IO;

procedure Introduction is
    InvoiceNumber : constant := 0000674

begin
    Put_Line ("Invoice          #:              "            &
integer' image (InvoiceNumber) );
    end Introduction;
```

Chapter 5 Boolean Variables and Enumerations

Boolean variables are variables that holds either True or False values. The keyword **Boolean** is used to declare variables a Boolean.

```
with Ada.Text_IO;
use Ada.Text_IO;

procedure Practice is
    IsCourteous : Boolean;

begin

end Exercise;
```

After declaring a new Boolean variable, its default value is False.

Showing Values

To show the Boolean variable's value, the input value is placed within the parentheses of Boolean'image().

```
with Ada.Text_IO;
use Ada.Text_IO;

procedure Practice is
    IsCourteous : Boolean;

begin
    Put_Line("Employee     is      courteous:      "     &
Boolean'image(IsCourteous));
    end Exercise;
```

The compiler will produce this result:

```
Employee is courteous: FALSE
```

Initializing

Initializing is specifying the Boolean variable's value. This is giving the Boolean variable a True or a False result when the program is carried out. In initializing, the value of the Boolean variable is transformed from the default False into something more specific and one that has more meaning.

```
with Ada.Text_IO;
use Ada.Text_IO;

procedure Practice is
   IsCourteous : Boolean := TRUE;

begin
   Put_Line("Employee     is     courteous:      "     &
Boolean'image(IsCourteous));

end Exercise;
```

The result is:

```
Employee is courteous: True
```

ENUMERATIONS

Enumerations refer to constant integers entered in a series, each having specific positions in the list. These enumerations are often easily recognized because they form a meaningful name or phrase. Using enumerations also limits use of numerals at the end of variable names. It also helps in being more specific and for easy understanding. For example, instead of using `Variable1`, `Variable2`, etc. In naming these, use enumerations such as `TypeofHouse, Q1Grades, Q2_Q3Sales`, etc.

Creating

To create an enumeration, start by entering the keyword type. Next, enter the enumeration's name and then a pair of parentheses (). The name for each item on a list is entered within these parentheses.

```
     type   Enumeration_Name   is   (Item1,   Item2,
Item_n);
```

For example:

```
with Ada.Text_IO;
use Ada.Text_IO;

procedure Exercise is
    type  ShoeTypes  is  (BalletFlats,  RunningShoes,
BasketballShoes, StilletoHeels);

begin


end Exercise;
```

Items in the enumeration are, by default, considered as constant integers.

The members of the enumeration can be created as characters. To do this, study this example:

```
with Ada.Text_IO;
use Ada.Text_IO;

procedure Practice is
    type  ShoeTypes  is  (BalletFlats,  RunningShoes,
BasketballShoes);
    type Genders is ('j', 'd', 'm');

begin

end Exercise;
```
Declaring

To declare enumerations,

```
with Ada.Text_IO;
use Ada.Text_IO;

procedure Practice is
    type  ShoeTypes  is  (BalletFlats,  RunningShoes,
BasketballShoes);
    type Genders is ('j', 'd', 'm');

    ShoeCategory : ShoeTypes;

begin

end Exercise;
```

Initializing

To initialize after an enumeration's declaration, specifying which item in the enumeration is assigned to a particular variable.

```
with Ada.Text_IO;
use Ada.Text_IO;

procedure Practice is
    type  ShoeTypes  is  (BalletFlats,  RunningShoes,
BasketballShoes);
    type Genders is ('j', 'd', 'm');

    ShoeCategory : ShoeTypes := BalletFlats;

begin

end Exercise;
```

To determine what value is currently held by a declared variable, command the compiler to display it. Use the enumeration's name and enter `image(). Type the variable name within the parentheses.

```
with Ada.Text_IO;
use Ada.Text_IO;

procedure Practice is
    type   ShoeTypes   is   (BalletFlats,   RunningShoes,
BasketballShoes);
    type Genders is ('j', 'd', 'm');

    ShoeCategory : ShoeTypes := BalletFlats;

begin
    Put_Line("Shoe            Type:            "            &
ShoeTypes'image(ShoeCategory));

    end Exercise;
```

The displayed result will be:

```
Shoe Type: BALLETFLATS
```

Chapter 6 Conditions in Ada Program

One of the most common programs in Ada, and in most other computer programming languages is making comparisons. Two variables are compared against each other by using the operator =. The basic formula is:

```
Value1 = Value2
```

The basic use of this equality operation is to determine if 2 variables have the same value. Often, one of these values is a variable and the other is a constant. The above syntax will command the compiler to compare the value held by the variable `Value1` against the value set for `Value2`. A true result is obtained if both values prove to be of the same value. The comparison has a false result if the values are different from each other.

```
with Ada.Text_IO;
use Ada.Text_IO;

procedure Exercise is
    value1 : Integer := 34;
    value2 : Integer := 78;
begin
    Put_Line("Value 1 = " & natural'image(value1));
    Put_Line("Value 2 = " & natural'image(value2));
    Put_Line("Comparison of value1 = 34 produces " &
boolean'image(value1 = 34));

end Exercise;
```

The displayed result after the compiler carries out this program is:

```
Value 1 = 34
Value 2 = 78
```

Comparison of value1 = 34 produces TRUE

Inequalities

Aside from equality operations, Ada also supports inequality procedures. This is when 2 values are being compared to find if they are not equal. Instead of using the = operator, use the binary operator `/=`.

```
Value1 /= Value2
```

Less Than

This operation is used in comparing 2 value to determine if one value is lower than the other. The operator used is <. The syntax is:

```
Value1 < Value2
```

The value of the variable `Value1` is compared against the value held by `Value2`. A positive or true result is obtained if `Value1` is lower than the value of `Value2`. Otherwise, the result will be false.

Less than or Equal to

This operation combines "equality" and "less than" operations. Here, 2 values are compared against each other to find out whether they are of the same value or the first declared value is lower than the second one. The <= operator is used for this condition, using the following syntax:

```
Value1 <= Value2
```

The operator <= carries out the comparison. If the values of both `Value1` and `Value2` variables are the same, the result is positive or true. If the operand on the left (`Value1`) has a value lower than the operand on the right (`Value2`), the result is positive or true. If the value of the left operand is higher than that of the right operand, the result is false.

Greater than

The operator > is used in determining if one value is higher or greater than the other. The syntax is

```
Value1 > Value2
```

In this case, both operands can be variables. Or, the right operand is constant and the left operand is a variable. A true (positive) result is obtained if the value of the operand on the left is higher than the value of the left operand. If not, the returned value will be false.

Greater than or Equal to

This operation combines "equality" and "greater than" operations. The operator used for this condition is >=, with the syntax:

```
Valu1 >= Value2
```

Value1 and Value2 are compared. If the values they hold are the same, the result is positive or true. If the value of the operand on the left (Value1) is higher than the value held by the right operand (Value2), the result is also true or positive. If the left operand's value is less than that of the right's, the result obtained is null or false.

Chapter 7 Creating a Program

First off, in creating a program, the most basic parts are the package, variable and the statement. A package is a source file where certain commands are stored. Some of these commands include print text and perform specific mathematical functions, among others. Variables are memory spaces where values can be stored. Values include characters, numbers, words or combinations of all these.

Basic Program Structure

Every program in Ada has the following basic structure:

```
with Package_Name; use Package_Name;

   procedure Program_Name is

     Variable : Some_Type;

   begin

     Statement_1;
     Statement_2;


   end Program_Name;
```

The name of this basic sample program is procedure.

The variable declaration is made in the line "`Variable : Some_Type;`". The term "`Some_Type`" is actually where the type of variable used in the program is defined. For example, if the value of the variable used in the program is an integer, this specific line will be written as "`Variable : Integer;`". If the value is a floating-point or a decimal, the line will be written as "`Variable : Float;`".

The semicolons placed at the end of statements or variable declarations are important. These allow programmers to place several statements or variable declarations all in a single line.

To start executing the actual program statements, write the begin statement.

The lines `Statement_1;` and `Statement_2;` do not necessarily mean anything. These are replaced by commands that actually do something when creating a real program.

The line end `Program_Name;` is placed to denote where the program ends.

For an actual sample basic program, the `Hello World` is the most common starting point in practicing how to make a program in any computer programming language.

```
with Ada.Text_IO;
use Ada.Text_IO;

    procedure Welcome_Programmer is

      -- no variables needed here :)

    begin

      Put ("Welcome Programmer");

  end Welcome_Programmer;
```

The name of the above procedure is "`Welcome Programmer`".

The addition of the statements "`with`" and "`use`" are important because these are used to call upon the `Text_IO` package so that it can be used in the program. `Text_IO` is an Ada package. It contains all the functions that support input/output operations. It is an important package especially for programs that involve displaying and gathering texts. The addition of "`Ada.`" to `Text_IO` is necessary in order to specify that the library used for this particular program is from Ada. The reason is that Ada has the ability to interface with several other programming languages. This addition helps in being more specific, which is what Ada is best known for.

This sample program actually does nothing other than printing the phrase "`Welcome Programmer`". And because of this, variable declarations are not required. The section where declarations are made is left blank. The double hyphen (--) is used when entering comments, such as the text "`No variables needed here`". Comments are text strings that the compiler ignores. These are mainly additional information to help in gaining a better understanding of the program and its code. The double hyphen before comments is absolutely necessary. Otherwise, the compiler will recognize the string of text as an attempt to use that string as a variable declaration. When the program is compiled, an error message will appear.

The line `Put ("Welcome Programmer");` is the one that executes the actual displaying or printing of the text phrase on the computer screen. The parentheses are important in this section because it tells the compiler what specific words should be printed.

A lot of the names in the above sample program start with uppercase characters (capital letters). For example, the package name `Text_IO;`. Writing in uppercase is not a requirement. It is mainly used to make the program code look more presentable. Even though it isn't a must, good programmers practice this.

After trying that simple program, here is a slightly more complex one. This following sample program requires the user to input the first name and then prints it, together with a few other texts.

```
with Ada.Text_IO; use Ada.Text_IO;

    procedure Write_Name is

        Name    : String (1..80);
        Length  : Integer;

    begin

        Put ("Enter first name> ");
        Get_Line (Name, Length);
        New_Line;
        Put ("Greetings ");
        Put (Name (1..Length));
        Put (", enjoy your experience with Ada!");


    end Write_Name;
```

So, `Text_IO;` is invoking the desired package that will execute this program. The name of this procedure is `Write_Name`. In the next line, "`Name : String (1..80);`", the variable is `Name`, which will

42

be the name that the programmer will input. The type indication is `String (1..80)`. This section signifies that for the variable `Name`, a string of characters consisting of a maximum of 80 characters can be entered. `Length` is the second variable in this program. This is of an integer type, which is used in remembering how many characters were actually entered into the program.

Running this program will display a message, "`Enter first name`". This signifies that the program is ready to accept input. Type the name and hit the Enter key. The program will then skip one line (from the statement "`New Line;`" in the program code. Then the program will complete its statements within its code and print the line:

```
      Greeting  (name),  enjoy  your  experience  with
Ada!
```

43

Chapter 8 ADA Packages

One of the most unique features of Ada programming language is its clearly defined, highly specific modularization system and its separate compilation features. Even with separate compilation, Ada is still able to maintain strong type checking between several compilations.

Benefits of packages in Ada

Packages are unique to Ada for these reasons:

- The contents of packages are placed in separate namespaces. This prevents naming collisions

- The details of package implementation may be hidden intently, called information hiding

- Object orientation needs to have a type defined, including the primitive subprograms within that same package.

- Separate compilation

Uses of packages

There are many uses for packages, such as:

- Creating groups of related subprograms. The shared data are included in this created group but the data will not be visible outside of the package.

- Manipulating one or several data types including their subprograms

- Instantiating generic packages under different conditions

Packages are primarily program units within the Ada language. These allow groups of logically associated entities, to be specified. A package typically contains declarations of a certain type, which is often a private extension or a private type. A package also includes the type's declarations of primitive subprograms. This can be initiated from outside of the package while Ada still hides the declarations' inner workings from any unauthorized or outside users.

Separate compilation

Bodies and declarations of packages are commonly coded into distinct files and then compiled separately. This will place the package at the level of the library, where it becomes accessible to all of the other codes when using the *with* statement. The package body can be divided into many different files. To do this, on or more of the subprogram implementations are specified as *separate*.

Strong type checking between the separate compilations is maintained through the enforcement of compilation order rules and checking compatibility.

Parts of an Ada package

There are 2 parts of a package, namely, package specification and package body. The package specification is further divided into logical parts, namely, the visible and the private part. The visible part is the only portion that is mandatory. Private part of the package specification is non-compulsory. Also, the package specification can exist without having a package body. The body only comes into existence if there are any incomplete items contained in the package. The body is designed to complete these incomplete items. If no incomplete declarations are present, there should not be any package bodies.

Package Specification- Visible Part

The package specification's visible part contains the description of all its subprogram specifications, types, variables, constants, and others. The information is visible to every user of the package, hence, the name.

For example:

```
package Public_Package is

      type Range_58 is range 1 .. 58;

end Public_Package;
```

The type Range_58 is of the integer type, numerous operations are implicitly declared within this particular package.

Package specifications- Private part

There are 2 primary purposes of the private part. These are:

- Completing deferred definitions of private constants and types

- Exporting entities that are visible only to the package's "children"

For example:

```
package Package_Private is

      type Private_Type is private;

private

      type Private_Type is array (1 .. 58) of Integer;

end Package_Private;
```

The type is a private one, clients and users cannot use this as long as the visible part does not contain any operations.

Package Body

The body contains the definition of the package's implementation. The package body must implement the subprograms that the package specification defines. Any new types, objects or subprograms can remain invisible to package users even if defined in the package body.

```ada
package Package_Containing_Body is

    type Basic_List is private

    procedure Set_B (This : in out Basic_List;
                        A_B : in         Integer);

    function Get_B (This : Basic_List) return Integer;
private

    type Basic_List is

        list

            B : Integer;

        end list ;

    pragma Pure_Function (Get_B; --not a standard pragma in Ada

    pragma Inline (Get_B);

    pragma Inline (Set_A);


end Package_Containing_Body;

package body Package_Containing_Body is


    procedure Set_B (This : in out Basic_List;

                            A_B : in     Integer)

    is

    begin

        This.B := A_B;

    end Set_A;


    function Get_B (This : Basic_List) return Integer is

    begin

        return This.B;

end Package_Containing_Body;
```

How to Use Packages

Naming the package using a "with" clause is necessary before it can be used. Naming a package in a "use" clause is needed if the goal is to have direct visibility of the particular package.

Standard with clause

Visibility of the public portion of a unit to the succeeding defined unit is provided for by a standard "with" clause. Imported packages may be used within any parts of a defined unit, which includes the body whenever the specification uses the clause.

Private "with" clause

This feature is only present in Ada 2005. The following example illustrates what this kind of "with" clause is and how it is used.

```
private with Ada.Strings.Unbounded;

package Private_With is
```

(Ada.Strings.Unbounded package will not be visible at this instance)

```
   type Basic_List is private;


   procedure Set_B (This : in out Basic_List;
                    A_B : in          String);


   function Get_B (This : Basic_List) return String;
private
```

The package (Ada.Strings.Unbounded) visibility begins at this point

```
package Unbounded renames Ada.Strings.Unbounded;


type Basic_List is

      list

        B : Unbounded.Unbounded_String;

      end list


pragma Pure Function (Get_A);

pragma Inline (Get_B);

pragma Inline (Set_B);


end Private_With;

package body Private_With is
```

The package "Private With" is now also visible.

```
procedure Set_B (This : in out Basic_List;

                   A_B : in        String)

is

begin

   This.B := Unbounded.To_Unbounded_String (A_B);

end Set_B;


function Get_B (This:Basic_List) return String is

begin

   return Unbounded.To_String (This.B);

end Get_B;


end Private _With;
```

Limited "with" clause

This is only present as a feature in Ada 2005. Consider the following example as how o use the limited type of "with" clause.

```
limited with Courses;

package Students is

    type Student is tagged private;

    procedure Assign_Student
        (S : in out Student;
         C : access Courses.Courses'Class);

    type Courses_Ptr is access all Course.Course'Class;

    function Current_Course (S : in Students) return Course_Ptr;
    ...
end Students;
limited with Students;

package Courses is

    type Courses is tagged private;

    procedure Choose_President
        (Course : in out Course;
         President : access Students.Student'Class);
    ...
end Courses;
```

How to Organize Packages

There are various ways of organizing packages. Some of the common ones include the following:

Nested packages

Nested packages are packages that have been declared inside another package. Just like a regular package, a nested package has a private and a public part. From the outside, items that have been declared within a nested package (N) will have the usual visibility features. Programmers may name these items with the use of full dotted names such as P.N.X.

```
package P is

    B: Integer;
```

This is a nested package;

```
        package N is

            X: Integer;

        private

            Foo: Integer;

        end N;


        C: Integer;

    private
```

This is another nested package

```
package M is

    Y: Integer;

private

    Bar: Integer;

end M;



    end P;
```

Within the package, visibility of declarations occurs during the introduction. This follows textual order. This means that the nested package N is only declared after the declaration B is made. Declaration E follows N and refers only to the items within the nested N package. Neither of these can refer nor look ahead of any of the declarations that occur after them.

Child packages

Child package is another unique Ada feature. It allows the extension of a unit or package's functionality to its "children" or "child packages". All of the parent's functionality becomes available to the child. All of the declarations, whether private or public, of the parent package will also become visible to all of its child packages. For example,

```
package Drawer is

    pragma Detailed_Body;


    type Label is range 10_000 .. 99_999;

        type Thing (Identifier : Label) is abstract tagged limited
null record:

        type Thing_Ref is access constant Thing'Class;


        function Next_Label return Label;
```

This will give a new Label for a Thing to Place in the Drawer.

```
        function compare (it : Thing; Text : String)

    return Boolean is abstract;
```

52

This checks whether It contains any bibliographic information that matches the Text.

This is Drawer manipulation.

```
procedure Place (it : Thing_Ref);

function Get (identifier : Label) return Thing_Ref;

function Search (title : String) return Label;


end Drawer;
```

The child package's name will contain the name of its parent unit, and then followed by the identifier of the child package, which will be separate by a dot to period (.).

```ada
with Ada.Strings.Unbounded; use
Ada.Strings.Unbounded;


package Drawer.Trinkets is


      type Ornaments is (

            Jewelry,

            Memorabilia,

            Correspondence,


      type Trinket (Kind : Ornaments; Identifier : Label) is new
Thing (Identifier)

            with record

                  Collected : Unbounded_String;

                  Date      : Unbounded_String;

            end record;


      function compare(it: Trinket; text: String) return Boolean;


end Drawer.Trinkets;
```

Chapter 9 What's New in Ada 2012

The latest version of the Ada programming language is Ada 2012. The most otable offer of this new version is its supportive capabilities for contract-based type of programming. This feature allows for more validation to codes that are mission-critical. This further increases the reliability of the program, which is already famous for being high compared all other programming languages.

Ada 2012 brings the highly specialized contract-based programming into mainstream programming. It used to be highly specialized and access to such programming type is limited. With Ada 2012, programmers can now specify the intent of their programs more clearly. This is made possible by subtype predicates, pre- and post-conditions, and type variants. As a result, software programmers can embed requirements right into the source codes. This feature also makes it much easier in reviewing and understanding programs. It also makes it even more convenient to verify through runtime checks, static analysis tools and/or compiler.

Contract-based programming

This newest version has been ISO-approved in December 2012. For most people, "new versions" tend to be a let-down. Most of "new versions" of anything- whether programming languages or any other product- usually advertise new and exciting features. But, in practice, these "new features" are not so helpful or life-changing. But, with Ada 2012, there is one feature that is "earth-shaking"- the contract-based programming. This feature is also called design by contract.

In the world of software, "contract" refers to the assertion of a program component's property. This reflects the requirement that should be met by that specific component. One example is the ability to set preconditions and post conditions in subprograms, which reflect the functions and procedures. For data types, there are predicates and invariants that can be used for contract-based programming needs.

The concept of contract-based programming isn't exactly new. What made it seem new is that Ada 2012 was able to incorporate this feature and used it in broader domains which involved high-reliability, security-critical and safety-critical programming. Ada has long been used for these kinds of programming but with the inclusion of this new feature, the resulting programs are more reliable and able to handle more critical requirements. For instance, a subset of Ada with high–integrity was used in developing England's newly set up iFacts Air Traffic Control program. In fact, Ada programming language is already widely used on both new civilian and military aircrafts because of the high specificity, reliability, safety and security capabilities.

A crucial element in improving the reliability of a program is the contract. By including it in the program, there is better confidence that the program will be able to correctly meet all its requirements every time.

In a general sense, the basic process of software development involves the following steps:

- High-level requirements are defined

- Low-level requirements are derived

- Design or architecture is formulated, which should meet all the requirements

- A code that will implement the design is finally written.

All these steps do not have to be carried out in this strict sequence. In fact, it is fairly common to make iterations and feedback throughout software programming.

Contracts basically act a bridge over the gap that often exists between the software's low-level requirements and its code. Some software can work just as well even without contracts, but with less efficiency, safety, security and reliability. With the gap sufficiently bridged, the software performs much better.

Contracts are also used in creating formal documentations about the relationship of the code to the defined and derived requirements. These help in giving a better and clearer information and understanding about the code and the program.

There are a number of contract types. The 2 most important ones are the preconditions and the postconditions of a subprogram. Preconditions have to be true upon entry while postconditions have to be true upon exit. These contracts are not entirely distinctive to Ada programming language. The use of contracts and their advantages have long been established. These are most appreciated in their use in creating formal proof for a program's correctness. What makes it seem to be a new and defining feature of the new Ada version is because other major computer programming languages, as of the present, have not yet fully incorporated contracts in their languages.

The incorporation of contracts changes the ways for using Ada when constructing highly reliable and large-scale software. Other languages do incorporate the use of preconditions and postconditions and programmers accustomed to these other programming languages may find it easy and familiar to work the new Ada feature. However, expect that Ada has also incorporated new twists supported by Ada's intrinsic design. Others who have not been using preconditions and postconditions before may need to learn and practice more. Overall, the techniques and capabilities supported by the contract-based programming in Ada 2012 is surely a huge advancement in the programming world.

Chapter 10 Understanding Pre- and Postconditions

To better understand preconditions and postconditions, study these examples. First, assume that a program needs to process several arrays composed of integers. One of the required operations is removing any elements that have been duplicated from the given array. To do this in Ada, the array type must be defined and a subprogram is created to do the required removal.

```
type Int_Array is array (Natural range <>) of Integer;
procedure Dedupe (Arr: in out Int_Array; Last : out
Natural);
```

In this program, the declaration `Int_Array` permits the use of different bounds to create different objects of that array type. Lower bounds include `Natural` range, which are any integers that are non-negative. If the `Arr` is considered an object and is of the type `Int_Array`, the bounds are set against the constructs of `Arr'First` and `Arr'Last`. `Arr'First` defines the lower bound while the `Arr'Last` defines the upper bound.

Now, suppose that the part `Dedupe` has to meet these requirements:

- On its entry, there is at least 1 duplicated element in the `Arr` parameter.

- On its exit, all the duplicates must no longer be included. Only duplicates must be removed and no new element should have been added. The `Last` parameter should show a newly defined upper bound.

To express these requirements, comments in plain English can be included the program's source code. Ada takes this further by allowing for more precision in declaring these requirements through the use of preconditions and postconditions.

```
procedure Dedupe (Arr: in out Int_Array; Last : out
Natural) with
   Pre => Has_Duplicates(Arr),
   Post => not Has_Duplicates( Arr(Arr'First .. Last) )
          and then (for all Item of Arr'Old =>
                      (for some J in Arr'First .. Last
=>
                         Item = Arr(J)))
                   -- Only duplicates removed
          and then (for all J in Arr'First .. Last =>
                      (for some Item of Arr'Old =>
                         Item = Arr(J)));
                   -- Nothing new added
```

The `Has_Duplicates` section is a helper function, which can be defined as:

```
function Has_Duplicates(Arr : Int_Array) return Boolean
is
   begin
      return (for some I in Arr'First .. Arr'Last-1 =>
                   (for some J in I+1 .. Arr'Last =>
Arr(I)=Arr(J)));
      end Has_Duplicates;
```

Ada 2012 introduces a quantification syntax for preconditions and postconditions. These allow for more precise specification of what `Dedupe` procedure will do but without constraining the method of implementation. The above example shows that on entry, the parameter's value to the `Arr'Old` subprogram can be indicated in the postcondition.

When writing in plain English to add comments to the program, precision and completeness can be a difficult challenge. But, achieving these is critical in order to allow the code to fully meet the low-level requirements. By using contracts to express the requirements, precision is forced and assured. The required analysis can help in teasing out any precondition or postcondition that may otherwise have been overlooked. For instance, in the above example, adding the terms "`nothing new added`" and "`only duplicates removed`" in the postcondition is crucial. These terms can easily be forgotten and becomes typical bugs in the program, which can destroy security and reliability.

How to use Preconditions and Postconditions

After learning how to include contracts in subprograms, next is learning how to use them. Ada supports 3 ways in how to use these contracts.

The first use is simple. Contracts can be simply used to replace the comments written in plain English language. This way, contracts act as guides to the human reader and facilitates better understanding. In this capacity, contracts function in the same way as English language comments. The difference is that contracts in this capacity have higher precision and are unambiguous compared to comments. Reading contracts in the source code may seem like reading regular comments of a subprogram to find out what it is supposed to do. The difference with contracts is that the abstractions are at higher levels. Also, these contracts provide specifications for everything, nothing more and nothing less. What they contain is all that can be expected.

The second method of using contracts gives the option to let the compiler turn the contracts into runtime checks. In this capability, testing programs are no longer confined to simply checking the results, it will now include verifying every entry and exit for each subprogram, which eventually checks that the code performs as it should. If either precondition or postcondition fails, a runtime exception is raised. Runtime exceptions are already well-defined in previous versions of Ada. It is greatly improved by the presence of contracts. When exceptions occur, the failed test is precisely identified. This makes the entire debugging process so much easier. These checks can also be removed, like all other runtime checks are, when building the final production is initiated. This option is often used when the program has safety-critical applications. An example is aircraft software, in which the verification process of the entire program gives great confidence that all the checks put into place will not fail. In this capacity, runtime checks are used so that they will not be needed once the software is already in use. Programmers use contracts in this capacity to check any runtime errors during the software development so that when the final version of the software is finished, runtime errors and checks will no longer be needed because reliability is already firmly established. In practical application, eliminating the checks for the final program build will eliminate a flashing message to the pilot when a precondition fail-a scenario that won't be of much help. In other applications, the checks may have to be installed in the final program build. This is most practical if the software application won't have any problem with the extra inefficiency. Enabling the runtime checks would likely result in a shutdown and an error message. An example of real world application of enabling these checks is in an ATM software. When runtime error is raised, the ATM shuts down and will not dispense any money. This is a more acceptable occurrence rather than run the risk of getting undetected errors and allow the machine to dispense incorrect amounts.

The third use for contracts is that it can be used for formal verification. The procedure `Dedupe` in the previous example incorporates a set of pre- and postconditions that are expressed in a quantificational logic method. This allows the programmer and his automated tools to gain a better understanding of the conditions and the code that puts this particular procedure into action. With formal verification, there is a guarantee that the postconditions in the code hold on exit as long as the preconditions does the same on entry. This is guaranteed if preconditions and postconditions are explicitly defined. In getting proofs of correctness, the vital element is identifying what has to be proven. Using contracts systematically allows for a precise answer to the question "What to prove". This also makes it possible to carry out the process of proving in a modular approach.

In the procedure `Dedupe`, proving correctness can be carried out in isolation. The caller will have to ensure that the set of preconditions are met. Ada takes all these processes and makes them even more convenient. Ada 2012 allows and supports the carrying out testing and proving of the code all in the same program. Contracts make this possible by serving as an effective boundary between these 2 processes.

Chapter 11 Other Types of Contracts in Ada 2012

Aside from the preconditions and postconditions used in subprograms, there are several other contracts supported by Ada 2012. Among the most advantageous ones are predicates and type invariants.

Predicates

Predicates on types are conditions that values of that type must always meet. One of the most valuable predicates in the ranges on scalar types, which has already been part of Ada since the first version, Ada 83.

```
Test_Score : Integer range 0 through 100;

Distance : Float range -100.0 .. 100.0;
```

This capability is not present in other popular programming languages such as Java, C and C++. This is extremely valuable because it improves a program's understandability and reliability. It is a very important capability and is not entirely new. In fact, this capability is already part of Pascal for at least 40 years. Other programming languages do not include this in their languages for some reason. The resulting consequences cannot be overlooked. For instance, in C programming language, a lot of the buffer overruns can be effectively avoided if C supports range constraints.

Incorporating and supporting range constraints play vital roles. However, the capability is limited to capturing only the contiguous subranges of the value space of a scalar type. This concept is generalized in Ada 2012 to improve its function. In this newest version, programmers are able to specify the arbitrary subsets of the value of that type through the inclusion of the subtype predicates.

The subtype predicates in Ada 2012 are available in 2 forms. These are Static_Predicate and Dynamic_Predicate. Employment of either of these forms depends on the nature of the expression used to define the predicate.

An example is this:

```
type Month is

    (Jan, Feb, Mar, Apr, May, Jun, Jul, Aug, Sep, Oct,
Nov, Dec);


subtype Long_Month is Month with

Static_Predicate => Long_Month in Jan | Mar | May | Jul
| Aug | Oct | Dec;


subtype Short_Month is Month with

Static_Predicate => Short_Month in Apr | Jun | Sep |
Nov;   >>


subtype Even is Integer with

Dynamic_Predicate => Even rem 2 = 0;
```

Checking the predicate is done on assignment, which corresponds to range constraints:

```
L : Long_Month := Apr;        -- Raises Constraint_Error

E : Even := Some_Func(X, Y); -- Check that result is
even
```

More compile-time checking is possible with static forms. To illustrate, look at the following case statement:

```
case Month_Val is

    when Long_Month => ...

    when Short_Month => ...

end case;
```

In this example, Feb will be detected as absent by the compiler. It isn't possible to check dynamic predicates at compile time. However, at runtime, violations are still detected. Generally, runtime checks are required by predicates. So, with this example, when a Month value is assigned to Short_Month variable, runtime check will verify that an appropriate value is present.

Type Invariants

The type invariant is another contract type presented by Ada 2012. Invariants are private types, which are roughly the same as "protected types" in Java and C++. This are viewed through 2 kinds of perspectives. One perspective is through the user or the client of the type. Access to the type is only through the subprograms that the type supplies. There is no access to the type's implementation details. The other perspective is through the package or module used in defining the private type. The code is given full access to the implementation details of the type.

Type invariants make sure that values visible to clients are the appropriate ones. Subprograms that use the type as a parameter are guaranteed that the appropriate values available to them are reliable. Clients do not have access to the internals of private types. Hence, the client cannot possibly corrupt the given value. But, no checks are applied inside the package implementation that defines the type. This capability has a vital role in practical applications. Consistency is important in a complex object after its construction, not during the intermediate stages in the process of its construction.

The private type interface in Ada adequately provides the partitioning need to meet the 2 requirements that seem to be conflicting. One requirement is guaranteed consistency of the values. The other requirement is that sometimes, such guarantees do not necessarily apply. Just like when working with preconditions and postconditions, both invariants and predicates have 3 possible uses. They can be used as formalized comments about the allowed values of the variables. They can be used in activating runtime checks, which are optional and can be used to make sure that the required values are indeed present. And, invariants and predicates can be used as proof of correctness that must formally present appropriate values that have been assigned.

Conclusion

Thank you again for purchasing this book!

I hope this book was able to help you to understand Ada and get you started on the basics of this programming language.

The next step is to start getting more familiar with this programming language and be on your way to developing amazing applications and programs.

Finally, if you enjoyed this book, please take the time to share your thoughts and post a review on Amazon. We do our best to reach out to readers and provide the best value we can. Your positive review will help us achieve that. It'd be greatly appreciated!

Thank you and good luck!

Check Out My Other Books

Below you'll find some of my other popular books that are popular on Amazon and Kindle as well. Simply click on the links below to check them out. Alternatively, you can visit my author page on Amazon to see other work done by me.

C Programming Success in a Day

Android Programming in a Day

C ++ Programming Success in a Day

Python Programming in a Day

PHP Programming Professional Made Easy

CSS Programming Professional Made Easy

Windows 8 Tips for Beginners

If the links do not work, for whatever reason, you can simply search for these titles on the Amazon website to find them.

Made in the USA
Lexington, KY
05 January 2017